MW00653766

LITTLE BOOK OF

DOLCE &
GABBANA

First published in 2024 by Welbeck
An Imprint of HEADLINE PUBLISHING GROUP

1

Cataloguing in Publication Data is available from the British Library

ISBN 978 1 80279 765 7

Printed and bound in China

HEADLINE PUBLISHING GROUP
An Hachette UK Company
Carmelite House
50 Victoria Embankment
London EC4Y 0DZ

www.headline.co.uk
www.hachette.co.uk

LITTLE BOOK OF

DOLCE &
GABBANA

The story of the iconic fashion house

JESSICA BUMPUS

WELBECK

CONTENTS

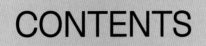

INTRODUCTION

Domenico Dolce and Stefano Gabbana are the creative minds behind the incredibly successful Dolce & Gabbana fashion house. For nearly 40 years, it has been known for a certain sort of high-octane glamour, deeply rooted in Sicilian style. Instantly recognizable, it offers an unmistakable blend of femininity, confidence and tradition: the Dolce & Gabbana muse is a strong, sensual woman.

I t should be noted there are only a handful of fashion brands whose names are universally known, and Dolce & Gabbana – much like Dior, Versace, Chanel, Armani and Vivienne Westwood – is one of them.

Theirs is not a label known only to the fashion elite. Instead their clothes are worn and adored by legions of fans – many of whom will fill the streets of Milan ahead of their shows (which are serious affairs, requiring passport identification to enter). And long before other fashion brands, they had established relationships with influencers.

OPPOSITE Emily Blunt wears Dolce & Gabbana for a photocall for *Oppenheimer*, in which she starred, on July 12, 2023.

The list of those who have worn Dolce & Gabbana on the red carpet is lengthy, which in itself goes to show what kind of brand this is – one that sparkles, shimmers and shines. Perfect for film stars, models and musicians from Helen Mirren, Emily Blunt, Mindy Kaling, Paul Dano and Keanu Reeves, to Kylie Jenner, Rosie Huntington-Whiteley, Alessandra Ambrosio, Kitty Spencer, Nicki Minaj, Ice Spice, Kylie Minogue and Madonna.

Indeed, the list goes on and on – and Beyoncé wore Dolce & Gabbana to perform on her 2023 Renaissance World Tour: a custom catsuit in black lace with a long skirt and opera cape in black tulle and black satin gloves; and a custom bodysuit in tulle with crystal rhinestones inspired by baroque artwork.

BELOW The designers with Naomi Campbell and Iman at the Met Gala 2001 celebrating the exhibition "Jacqueline Kennedy: The White House Years" at the Metropolitan Museum of Art Costume Institute.

LEFT Lily Donaldson on the D&G A/W 2009/10 catwalk.

OVERLEAF A memorable catwalk moment, S/S 2010, with Lily Donaldson, Natasha Poly and Karlie Kloss among the models.

OPPOSITE Cabbages and roses for S/S 2018.

RIGHT The pyjama collection for S/S 2009.

OVERLEAF An Alta Moda moment – this time the small town of Alberobello, in Bari (southern Italy), is transformed into an open-air catwalk.

Despite starting out from humble beginnings – with hardly any money and a few setbacks – Dolce & Gabbana is a brand that is used to rubbing shoulders with the stars. Early on, a relationship was born with the supermodels, who would come to epitomize the designers' sexy blend of dressing, which at its core is built on dedicated craftsmanship.

Vanity Fair Italia recently put 21 supermodels on its cover, all dressed in Dolce & Gabbana as if capturing a moment rewound, relived. The pieces – tight little dresses, bras and corsets (which at one point all the models wanted to wear on the catwalk) – had all stood the test of time, such are the classic but distinct codes to which the designers work.

It is an ability to tap into tradition as well as embrace innovation that has set the brand apart. And a quick scroll of the brand's Instagram will reveal the breadth of the designers' creative work. As well as heritage-inspired and homeware collections, they have created childrenswear, menswear, fragrance and jewellery – and even a couple of singles along the way. And they're keen to support emerging talent.

Over the years this body of work has been documented in many an article; there are countless reviews and various coffee table books: *10 Years of Dolce & Gabbana*, showing off their starry career; *20 Years: Dolce & Gabbana*, a glorious depiction of their collections featuring sketches and archive imagery; and *Animal*, in homage to their favourite animal prints; there are also tributes such as *Vogue on: Dolce & Gabbana* and *Dolce & Gabbana (Fashion Memoir)*.

And even though it debuted in another era, Dolce & Gabbana is a brand for the Instagram age, from its designs to its ethos.

As they have progressed through the years, the duo have drilled down more and more into the essence of what their

OPPOSITE The designers taking a bow at the end of their S/S 2024 menswear show.

OVERLEAF Dolce & Gabbana's Alta Moda spectacle takes place in Pretoria Square in Palermo, Sicily, 2017.

label is all about, able now to mine their own overflowing archives, seen pertinently in the Spring/Summer 2024 womenswear show – tailoring, lingerie, black and white, leopard print.

Of course, it has not been all plain sailing and there have been some controversies along the way – including campaigns and comments that have left the reputation of both brand and designers far from glittering. But part of their impressive CV is also that they have moved with the times, especially technology. And they have charmed with exuberant summer prints, princess dresses, stunning finales and spectacular sets – and an ode to their home, Italy. Which is where it all began.

OPPOSITE Ode to Italy, always, S/S 2016.

BELOW Bianca Brandolini d'Adda on the set of a Dolce & Gabbana campaign, October 2012, in Taormina, Sicily.

THE EARLY
YEARS

THE FAMOUS FASHION DESIGNER DUO

How Domenico Dolce and Stefano Gabbana came to meet is
now one of those fabled fashion stories, told over and over,
with something of a serendipitous charm about it.

One day while working at Giorgio Correggiari, a
highly regarded Italian fashion designer in Milan,
Dolce, then 23, answered the phone. At the other
end of the line was Gabbana, 19, enquiring about a job.

It was 1981 and, according to his account of events in the
coffee-table tome *20 Years: Dolce & Gabbana*, Gabbana had
been given the number for Giorgio Correggiari by a friend.
As the book *Vogue on: Dolce & Gabbana* tells it, the pair
then arranged to meet at a nightclub called No Ties, where
Correggiari was throwing a party.

Gabbana recalls going in for an appointment at which he
confessed that he had no real experience in fashion – it was
actually graphic design that he had studied – but Dolce took

OPPOSITE A portrait of Domenico Dolce and Stefano Gabbana taken in
the 1980s – the surroundings are suitably opulent.

him under his wing. He took a chance on the younger man,
teaching Gabbana how to sketch.

Dolce & Gabbana, as they would later be known, would
go on to have a personal relationship (which would end in the
early 2000s). By 1982, they were sharing an apartment from
which they were also doing freelance work for other companies,
including Marzotto, the Italian textile manufacturer, and Max
Mara, the Italian fashion brand known for its classic, camel-
coloured coats. There was also a short period of mandatory
military service for Gabbana. But soon, Dolce & Gabbana, the
brand, made its debut.

But before they became Dolce & Gabbana, they were
individually Domenico Dolce and Stefano Gabbana. A Leo and
a Scorpio, from the south and from the north, respectively.

Dolce was born in the town of Polizzi Generosa, Sicily, in
1958. His father was a tailor and his mother ran a haberdashery

store, which meant he grew up surrounded by fabrics. It is perhaps no surprise, then, that he would end up working in fashion – though he would long resist referencing his Sicilian heritage.

In *20 Years: Dolce & Gabbana*, celebrating the 20th anniversary of the brand and edited by the journalist Sarah Mower, Dolce details memories of his father's tailoring business: it had 30–40 employees at a time when there were two distinct styles of clothing. Clothes for people who worked in the country, and clothes for the gentry. What also stood out to him was the quality of the fabric. He remembers playing with fabric as a child, not toys, and apparently made his first pair of trousers aged 7, in miniature.

By the 1970s, his father adapted the business to modern times and introduced machinery. Until this point, Dolce had already learned everything the traditional way, by hand. It was the influence of his father, who was fascinated by fabric, that probably led the brand to use what is now a signature fabric of theirs, pinstripe. And at that time in their career, the early 1980s, the masculine fabric stood out among the era's loose and relaxed linens, its soft silhouettes.

Dolce had moved to Milan from Sicily to attend Istituto Marangoni, the school of fashion and design, but stayed only a year and a half because he was eager to get a job and work.

Gabbana, meanwhile, was born in 1962 in Milan. His family is from Venice, Veneto, and his father was a printer while his mother ironed clothes in a laundry. According to an interview with *Harper's Bazaar,* when he was really young he had dreams of being an actor, but he studied graphic design and went to work in the industry for six months. He soon realized it was not for him. Instead, he liked fashion. He didn't really know anything about it, other than what he liked.

This included Fiorucci, a youthful culture-based Italian brand (whose popularity has recently been reprised after a somewhat rocky road); the denim label Levi's; and Ray-Ban, notably its sunglasses. He also bought second-hand clothes from America. As reference points, these make a lot of stylistic sense for Gabbana, who is known for his love of colour, glamour and print; and a youthful, fun street style would populate their secondary line, D&G, a diffusion range they would design throughout the 1990s and 2000s.

Gabbana recalls that by the end of the 1970s and early 1980s, fashion itself was becoming fashionable in Italy, both as an industry and a pastime. Milan was a manufacturing hub, producing some of the biggest fashion names, among whom Stefano and Domenico would soon be a part. There was also an energy in the city, especially when it came to the night life. The duo's routine would soon comprise late nights, early mornings, clubbing and working, working and clubbing; they worked very hard and the energy clearly fuelled them.

Their career together began with a label called Donna, Donna (it is supposed to be a play on Dolce's initials). Reportedly, it went down well with press and buyers to the extent that they started to speak to a factory about production. But a deal seems to have fallen through – the rumour is that the factory was put off by someone at an established label who had been dismissive of the enterprise. That was the end of Donna, Donna.

The inception of their own label, however, came about a little by chance. It was in 1985 that the late Beppe Modenese, who was often referred to as Italy's Prime Minister of Fashion, decided he wanted to give young designers a chance to showcase as part of what was by now a well-established event, full of big names. He would offer a slot at the end of the week.

Dolce & Gabbana – the duo came up with the label's eponymous name by looking at the inscription above their doorbell – was selected alongside two others. It was all quite last-minute, but a thrill to know their names would be up there with the best of the day: Giorgio Armani, Gianfranco Ferré, Gianni Versace. They had three months and £850, which then translated as two million lire, to design their first collection.

The collection was called Geometrissimo, for the Spring/ Summer 1986 season, and was shown at Milan Fashion Week in October 1985. Apparently over 600 people saw it.

Dolce had been inspired by the Japanese designers of the time, including Rei Kawakubo of Comme des Garçons, who had a love for volume and a more conceptual way of dressing. For context, it was power dressing – big shoulders, small skirts and a *take me seriously* attitude – that dominated fashion at this time, especially in Italy.

And indeed to look back on this early collection – and the couple of others that immediately followed too – can at times feel a little like looking at a completely different brand. Cocoon curves where silhouettes now are svelte. Stretch and jersey shapes, cut to be, as the name suggests, geometric. Hybrid pieces that looked like two garments but were actually one. Billowing and draped shapes in a palette of black, beiges and neutrals. No decoration, no embroidery, no sparkle or exuberant colour. No corsets, no bras.

The designers recall that the collection received good press, but the manufacturer – just like before – pulled out. Calls to others for help came to nothing. The collection seemed to be too extreme, the opposite of what was currently en vogue. It seemed like something once again wasn't on their side. However, thankfully, fate, luck and family would be.

That Christmas, Dolce returned home and told his family what had happened. It was his brother-in-law who suggested the family make the collection with their business – though in the wake of the production company pulling out, Dolce

OVERLEAF The pair pose for a portrait in New York, 1992.

thought he had cancelled the fabric order too. Fortuitously, the letter he sent never reached the company and they could in fact produce the collection after all. And so Dolce & Gabbana, the brand, could finally begin.

There would even be a next collection, titled Real Women, for the Autumn/Winter 1986/87 season. Of course, there would be many more collections, and Spring/Summer 2024, almost 40 years later, was an ode to grace, allure and the trademark codes of the Dolce & Gabbana woman, confident and seductive in sleek silhouettes, satin, lace and lingerie inspired by the 1960s.

They were one of the earliest working fashion designer duos, and certainly today they are probably the best known. The key to their success has, over the years, been put down to how the work is divided. Dolce is keen on details and perfecting things; he does the cuts, the shapes, the lines. Gabbana is concerned with the first impression, the feel and flair. Dolce dislikes colour and print; Gabbana loves them. Dolce is thought to have been more involved with the menswear; Gabbana with the youthful D&G line. They meet in the middle, a balance of what each other is not.

But that first season had been a close shave. Dolce's family also made their second collection which, as before, had been put together on very little money and with the generosity of friends from whom they borrowed accessories to bring together the styling, and who modelled the collection. They were a mix of actors and artists, dancers and architects and university lecturers. The result made the collection all the more authentic, women dressing how they would in real life in a mix of labels beside Dolce & Gabbana's clothes designs – which continued in a similar vein aesthetically to the previous collection.

Stretchy and voluminous, these were designs that experimented with technical fabrics and explored distressing denim (achieved with a pumice stone). Cocoon shapes were still key, the real women and the real accessories gave it a strong sense of grounding, but it is easy to agree with the designers who have admitted that these clothes weren't quite them: weren't Dolce & Gabbana as we know it today, not quite yet. The designers were still a little minimal.

Next came Trasformismo, their third collection for Spring/ Summer 1987. And by now, word among the fashion industry had started to get around about the pair of designers. Press and buyers packed into the showroom to see this new label whose star was on the rise. Browns, the much-loved and famous London store that had also launched the career of John Galliano (and would do the same later for Alexander McQueen and Hussein Chalayan), was there too.

BELOW Domenico Dolce and Stefano Gabbana in New York City on October 24, 1996.

OVERLEAF Taking a bow at the end of their menswear show for S/S 1992.

These were clothes that explored the idea of transformation; clothes that could be worn lots of different ways but which had been created in Italian fabrics. This combination of old with the new, tradition with innovation, would become a recognizable trait of their work throughout their career.

A short profile featured in *Vogue Italia* in January 1987; and Browns ended up buying the collection. Not only had the collection struck a chord with press and buyers but it had also begun to reveal Dolce's Sicilian roots. The collection was photographed in Pantelleria, an island in the Strait of Sicily in the Mediterranean.

They would further look to Dolce's native Sicily for the next collection, Autumn/Winter 1987/88's Sicily, a turning point for the brand. Here were cardigans, black and white, shawl-like jackets, shirts and draped balloon-hem skirts. This is, arguably, where we start to see the solid flourishes that have come to define the brand as it recognizably is today.

Dolce has spoken about how he originally went to Milan to escape Sicily and how it was Gabbana who encouraged him to embrace his Sicilian heritage – its craft and techniques, and its culture. A culture that Gabbana loved, and one that Dolce would soon embrace.

After those first few seasons, the idea of Sicily, their Italian heritage, and Dolce & Gabbana would take shape. As would the importance of another of the country's exports in their design world: the cinema of Neorealism.

OPPOSITE One of the several Dolce & Gabbana stores in London, 2021.

CINEMA AND SICILY: THE DOLCE DREAM

THE INFLUENCE
OF THE GOLDEN AGE

There are two recurring and inextricably linked influences
that underpin the design universe of the Dolce & Gabbana
label: cinema and Sicily. The latter, of course, is the southern
slice of Mediterranean Italy from where Dolce hails.

P icturesque landscapes of beautiful blue skies,
rolling mountains and hills, ancient architecture,
and a culture steeped in history. And the impact
of the former can in many ways be seen in pretty much
everything the duo has ever done – early on, Fabrizio Ferri
photographed the model (now actress) Amira Casar wearing
pieces from their Trasformismo collection in the ancient
surrounds of Pantelleria, on its historic streets with the
white sheets hung out and billowing behind her – a sight so
familiar to southern Italy.

OPPOSITE The spirit of Sicily has always run through the designers'
collections. Here, for S/S 2018.

OVERLEAF Recent shows, increasingly, have gone back to Dolce's
Sicilian roots. Here, menswear A/W 2020/21.

Even the tale of their meeting has something of a film's storyline to it. The moody and evocative campaign imagery has also often felt cinematic, as though they are stills lifted directly from a film classic. Those created by Steven Meisel, a long-term collaborator over the many years, have particularly stood the test of time, becoming iconic fashion imagery in their own right. They have also become integral to the whole ethos of the Dolce & Gabbana world: nostalgia, a romantic way of life, aspiration, glamour.

Then, of course, there are the shows themselves. These have featured elaborate sets, more spectacular over the years – including a whole market with stalls and fresh produce – to cater for a new lens: social media. Dramatic finales with storms of models marching down the catwalk – often all dressed in the same look, or variants of it – have become a brand signature as well as a much-anticipated highlight of Milan Fashion Week, and really pack a punch that underlines what the brand is all about.

Which leads us back once again to Sicily, Domenico Dolce's place of birth.

To think of Sicily, after all, is to think rather wistfully of escape: be that to its history and to a different pace and way of life; or to its sun, sea, beauty, character and charm. Sicily has proved to be a hugely valuable source of inspiration over the years and, more importantly, acted as a unique selling point to counteract the prevailing fashions when Dolce & Gabbana were starting out. As trends came and went, Sicily has always been there as an inspiration, and it will always be theirs.

Dolce had intended to come to Milan to get away from the past, from Sicily, thinking the city was an answer to his craving for modernity. But on holiday in Palermo, following their Spring/Summer Trasformismo collection, Gabbana saw a

OPPOSITE A couple on holiday in Sicily, circa 1950–60.

OVERLEAF Dolce and Gabbana are known for their dramatic and theatrical catwalk presentations. Here, S/S 2018.

RIGHT The traditional white vest and cap combination, Dolce & Gabbana, A/W 2020/21.

photograph that felt very Sicilian to him. And very much like the image he wanted to create: sensual and black and white. (It all starts to make sense …)

What had caught Gabbana's eye was the work of Ferdinando Scianna, a Magnum photographer known for his street photography, not his fashion photography. The designers got in touch with him, showed him their clothes and explained to him their love for Sicily, and Scianna – himself Sicilian – agreed to shoot with them. They shot the collection in Palermo on the model Marpessa Hennink, photographing among the real local people as they went about their day in the markets as well – just as the cinema of Italian Neorealism had also documented the lives of everyday people, often Sicilians. The designers later

BELOW Italian film director and screenwriter Roberto Rossellini, often considered the father of Italian Neorealism, and his wife, Swedish actress Ingrid Bergman, during a break in filming for *Stromboli* on Scari Beach on the island of Stromboli, off the north coast of Sicily.

noted that it made sense, for their purposes then, not to involve a fashion photographer – and they were right.

The resulting images are striking, moody and black and white, and feature their jersey designs in long and twisted shapes. The sensual and romantic fashion contrasts beautifully to the real-life backdrop. This was the beginning of a developing relationship with Neorealism for the duo, who found themselves inspired by its distinct visual language, its styling details and its actresses – especially the way they wore their clothes in the films.

Neorealism is deemed a golden age of cinema in Italy.

RIGHT Ingrid Bergman on location outside Naples with Roberto Rossellini, filming *Viaggio in Italia*.

It grew out of the aftermath of the Second World War when Italian filmmakers were determined to tell the stories of ordinary people whose lives had been impacted by the conflict. These were not the glossy and glamorous big-budget productions from Hollywood. Instead, they were the reverse: localized, gritty and, as the name would imply, real. And in many ways, therefore, modern.

Among the foremost directors of the movement was Roberto Rossellini, the father of the model and actress Isabella Rossellini – she would go on to become a friend of Dolce and Gabbana and work with them on and off the catwalk. Roberto is widely thought of as being the father of the genre; his fellow Neorealist directors include Vittorio De Sica, Luchino Visconti and Giuseppe De Santis.

ABOVE 1949, Ingrid Bergman with Roberto Rossellini on the set of the film *Stromboli*. Dolce & Gabbana's campaigns often mimicked similar idyllic and cinematic scenes.

Following this exploration for the Sicily collection, they went one step further for the Spring/Summer 1988 collection, The Leopard, inspired by Luchino Visconti's film of the same name. Exploring the idea of beauty and contrasts in wealth, this is the collection that features their first bra and slip.

A campaign was once again photographed with Scianna and they even went so far as to go to the same location as Visconti had for his film, Villa Gangi, and to Palermo's markets, to create the feeling of tradition and Italian-ness.

The collection features a lot of black – petticoat skirts, little crisp over-shirts and demure dresses, each with the appearance of an old world, understated undergarment. All bear the undeniable charm and romance of Sicily – hallmarks in the making.

Autumn/Winter 1988/89 is when further signature styles and designs became apparent, including the well-known pinstripe.

OPPOSITE Italian director Luchino Visconti stands beside the camera and looks from above a scene from the film The Leopard, 1963.

BELOW The cinema of Italian Neorealism has provided inspiration for the designers, from its actresses to its films, such as The Leopard, seen in production here in 1962. Director Luchino Visconti sits behind the camera; to his right sits the film's star, Burt Lancaster.

Shawls, velvet, caps and waistcoats further contributed to the look.

Their next collection would continue to draw from this world of devoted Sicilian nostalgia. Spring/Summer 1989, La Targa Florio, included corset tops to full dresses, crochet, white pinstripe, lace, svelte silhouettes, shirting and crochet. It would also cement their identity and direction as a brand – a hit first with the British, then the Americans and lastly, they say, the Italians.

Dolce and Gabbana began to collaborate with the acclaimed photographer Steven Meisel for the Autumn/Winter 1989/90 collection, The Forties. And it was at his suggestion that they worked with Isabella Rossellini. This would be the start of a fruitful relationship between all parties. Rossellini would walk in shows, feature in campaigns and go on to write the introduction to the book celebrating their 10th anniversary. In it, she highlights their unique blend of tradition and innovation, explains how she enjoyed wearing their pinstripes and describes her memory of the first thing of theirs she ever wore: a white shirt cut to show off her breasts. Another story well told.

At the shoot, which took place in New York, Gabbana likened Isabella to the Italian actress Anna Magnani, who starred in the Neorealist film *Bellissima* as well as *The Rose Tattoo*. The designers would find themselves also borrowing from Anna Magnani's wardrobe styling: twinsets, unbuttoned shirts, bags and oversized coats. It was these real elements that fascinated them – and this is probably one of the reasons the brand was able to be such a success, always with one foot in reality as well as fantasy. Rossellini, meanwhile, also aligned well with the brand: as an Italian she was familiar with the area where Dolce had grown up and the magic of Italy, its culture and heritage.

OPPOSITE The actress Anna Magnani has inspired the duo. Here in *The Golden Coach* (1952).

RIGHT From the film *Too Bad She's Bad* (1954), Sophia Loren, another Dolce & Gabbana muse, and the actor and director Vittorio De Sica.

OPPOSITE Tailoring, here for A/W 2018/19, plays a significant role in the Dolce & Gabbana wardrobe and is a nod to Dolce's Sicilian heritage.

It is in this collection that Dolce & Gabbana gets sexier: Anna Magnani and Sophia Loren were often cited among muses throughout their careers, and the designs here are more obviously *look at me*. In a bustier corset encrusted with beads Rossellini plays the perfect Dolce & Gabbana woman.

Other Neorealist muses of note included the character Angelica Sedara, from *The Leopard*, with her full skirts and jewelled hair accessories. Sophia Loren, a muse to this day, became part of the Dolce & Gabbana world more officially in 2015 when she was given her own shade of red lipstick, Sophia Loren No 1. She has also featured in their adverts and been a guest of honour at their shows.

As the duo headed towards the 1990s, a heyday for the brand, their relationship with cinema would evolve once more. No longer would it just serve as inspiration; it would now become a means to show off their designs – on the red carpet and the stars who wore them. And it still is – a quick scroll of Instagram goes to show that. The brand has also moved with the times, being one of the first big fashion brands to openly welcome influencers and bloggers to its shows when others were unsure. (Indeed, their decision caused controversy among the fashion press.)

The late Franca Sozzani, the renowned editor of *Vogue Italia*, made a pertinent observation about the duo: that they have the ability to turn women into stars. Indeed, they seemed to have an in-built camera lens.

For the British *Vogue* cover (their first) of August 1992, Geena Davis, one of the stars of *Thelma & Louise*, wore a black lace Dolce & Gabbana body and sat, appropriately, on a leopard-

OPPOSITE Madonna attends a Dolce & Gabbana show in 1992 – the pair became firm friends with the pop star.

BELOW Holding back the crowds during a Dolce & Gabbana show in 1992.

print pouf; leopard print has also become one of their signatures.

Their connection with Hollywood, fame and celebrities was strengthening. Madonna was snapped on the front row. They met in 1989, and she would go on to be one of their biggest and starriest champions. She remains very much a fan to this day – the brand posted an image of her wearing one of their kaftans while she celebrated her birthday in August 2023. In 1989, she was filming *Dick Tracy* in New York and had already been spotted wearing one of their designs – her picture was in the *International Herald Tribune*. So the duo contacted her to offer more pieces for her to wear. They ended up having dinner together and then went clubbing, and a friendship was made.

She then wore a jewelled body and black stockings by Dolce & Gabbana to the 1991 New York premiere of her documentary, *In Bed with Madonna*. She and the brand were an ideal match. Both masters of provocation, with a slight hint of rebellion and ambition, and both making use of religious iconography, sex and

LEFT Looking very Dolce & Gabbana is Gina Lollobrigida, one of their muses, in a publicity portrait for the film *Woman of Rome*, 1954.

their Italian heritage. Madonna would go on to wear custom pieces for The Girlie Show, her fourth tour, and later appeared in advertising campaigns.

The world of fashion and celebrity would become an especially important one over the next decade. The 1990s was the era of the supermodels. At the time akin to major film stars or performers, they were a new generation of young, glamorous stars who came with serious clout.

Dolce and Gabbana began their relationship with them around the time of the Autumn/Winter 1990/91 Little Italy collection. The photographer Steven Meisel introduced

them to Linda Evangelista and Christy Turlington, who both subsequently featured in a campaign that also included their new menswear offering (just launched). The images were once again cinematic and evocative.

OPPOSITE
Fashionable and film star friends: Linda Evangelista with Kyle MacLachlan, her former partner, at a party thrown by Dolce & Gabbana, 1995.

And they would become even more so for the next collection, Spring/Summer 1991's Love, which made pin-ups once again of Italian actresses Monica Vitti and Gina Lollobrigida via Linda Evangelista.

The collection for Autumn/Winter 1991/92 was in fact all about pin-ups, and its campaign captured the dazzling glamour of 1950s Hollywood. It channelled all the big names of the day, such as Marilyn Monroe and Elizabeth Taylor, while cleverly using the stars of the moment, notably Sherilyn Fenn, who was among the cast of David Lynch's mystery drama series hit *Twin Peaks.*

The collection was full of starlet sparkle, bustiers and corsets, jumpsuits and leopard print, stretchy and lithe: film-star glamour, heroines of their day reborn. It was old world, but it was also new world.

It would be the next collection that had the supermodels lining up to be a part of the Dolce & Gabbana world: Spring/Summer 1992, La Dolce Vita – and for the designers, it really was.

In another fabulous fashion tale, Linda Evangelista called up the rest of the supers to model the collection, though Dolce had to point out they had no budget to pay them. No matter: they paid with clothes. And apparently, on the catwalk, every one of them – Carla Bruni and Helena Christensen, to name just two – wanted to wear a corset. The finale saw them all in towels, as though just stepping from the bath or shower, with their initials on the back. Now that would have been a viral moment today.

Madonna would wear a lot of this collection, the campaign for which starred Isabella Rossellini and Monica Bellucci. It was photographed in a 1950s club in New York and the designers

LEFT Lizzo attends the 65th GRAMMY Awards on February 5, 2023 in Los Angeles wearing custom Dolce & Gabbana, including a sumptuous cape.

OPPOSITE Madonna at Madison Square Garden, New York, for The Girlie Show, in which she wore Dolce & Gabbana.

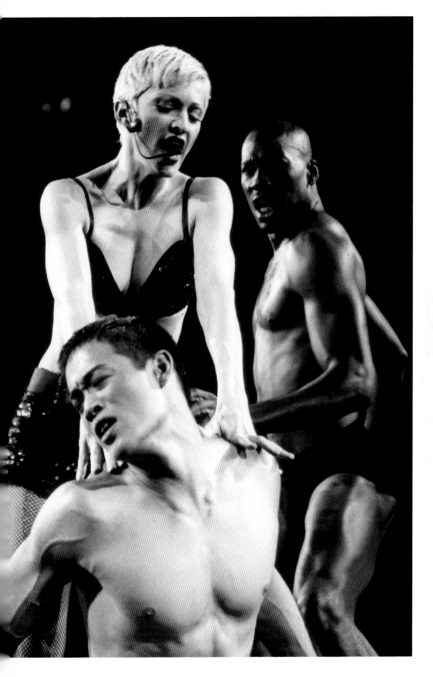

66 CINEMA AND SICILY: THE DOLCE DREAM

RIGHT Paul Dano
attends the 28th
Annual Critics Choice
Awards, 2023.

OPPOSITE *Emily
in Paris*'s Lucien
Laviscount attends
Cannes Film Festival,
2023, dressed in
Dolce & Gabbana.

have compared the production of it to making their own film – there are extras, there is dancing on tables; there are in-your-face bras, there is sultry eyeliner. The resulting images are once again captivating and just as though from a film. Sexy and fun, a little outrageous and raucous. This cinematic quality would come to dominate their campaigns into the millennium, even when their collections had begun to explore a world outside Sicily.

There were a couple of more bohemian and eclectic collections after La Dolce Vita: The Trip in Autumn/Winter 1992/93 and The Seventies in Spring/Summer 1993. From the latter, Madonna wore a patchwork piece for The Girlie Show tour. That season she also attended their show in Milan while promoting her *Erotica* album.

Autumn/Winter 1993/94 went down a Victorian path, featuring military coats and tapestry waistcoats, and was a mix of masculine and feminine – long skirts in chiffon and lace.

The following collection, Spring/Summer's Mediterraneo, vaguely tapped into the era's love for grunge and minimalism, but the Italian actress Monica Vitti would provide inspiration once again for the next collection, the Sicilian-infused Autumn/Winter 1994/95 New Rock 'n' Roll, full of leopard print and confidence.

Hollywood Glamour for Spring/Summer 1995 underlined that they had identified rich seams – cinema and Sicily – to create a potent blend, albeit with a little bit of kitsch thrown in. Isabella Rossellini and Brooke Shields would star in the campaigns.

In 1996 the duo published a book celebrating their 10-year anniversary, dedicated to everyone who had believed in them. Striking images depict their designs on the stars of Hollywood and fashion – both worlds of which they were now firmly a part. And the *Vogue* editor Anna Wintour wishes them well, noting she looks forward to decades more of their clothes.

The next few collections would still have one foot very much in

film: Spring/Summer 1996's Aeolian influenced by Michelangelo Antonioni's 1960s film *L'Avventura*; and the Autumn/Winter 1996/97 Fellini/*Le Notti di Cabiria*. It is in this later collection that Dolce's tailoring and Gabbana's colourful prints first combine, and the designers became the masters of mix.

In 2012, the duo decided to debut a couture line called Alta Moda. Each show – for selected press and an even more select clientele – is held in Italy. And the sweeping fantastical ballgowns seem fit for their own glorious costume drama, creations showing off brilliant craft techniques. These are sets and collections that are perhaps the most cinematic of all.

ABOVE Designers Domenico Dolce and Stefano Gabbana at the finale of their A/W 1994/95 show with actress Isabella Rossellini – daughter of the Neorealist film director, Roberto.

OPPOSITE The designers have always known how to tap into pop culture. Here, singer Machine Gun Kelly stands between the duo at the menswear A/W 2022/23 collection, at which he performed.

RIGHT Gwyneth Paltrow wears Dolce & Gabbana to the premiere of the film *A Perfect Murder*, 1998.

OVERLEAF Ashley Graham at the 76th Cannes Film Festival, 2023, wearing Dolce & Gabbana.

THE 1990s

A HEYDAY
FOR THE BRAND

By the early 1990s, Domenico Dolce and Stefano Gabbana
had established themselves in Milan's fashion scene and had
made substantial inroads internationally.

They began the decade with a bout of expansion: the launch of a menswear line; a fragrance, named Dolce & Gabbana, debuted in 1992; and, according to *Vogue*'s chronicles of the duo, the brand boasted a turnover of over $62 million – they had two stores to their name in Milan circa 1992 and one in Tokyo as well as 350 wholesale accounts. In autumn 1993 they signed a six-year partnership deal with the manufacturer Ittierre S.p.A to produce a diffusion line named D&G.

Diffusion lines, not so common today, were a less expensive and typically more youthful offering to accompany a main fashion line. Many of them would still have their own standalone shows and stores and while they were still part

OPPOSITE Cindy Crawford in an iconic Dolce & Gabbana look from
La Dolce Vita, S/S 1992.

OPPOSITE
Supermodel Cindy
Crawford in another
iconic Dolce &
Gabbana look
from La Dolce
Vita, S/S 1992.

BELOW Madonna
has worn looks
from Dolce &
Gabbana collections
throughout her
career. Here, on
The Girlie Show
tour, 1993.

of the overall brand universe, they targeted a slightly different, or emerging, customer. Over the last decade they have fallen a little out of favour – arguably replaced by the rise of the designer collaboration, from high street to adjacent industries. Dolce & Gabbana, for example, has a collaboration line with Smeg. They have produced beautiful fridges hand-painted with elements typical of puppet theatre and the Sicilian Cart, as well as toasters, coffee machines, kettles, blenders and mixers.

Fashion's road ahead, meanwhile, would explore minimalist and grunge terrain, neither of which was especially Dolce & Gabbana – not that it really mattered. The 1990s were arguably a heyday for the brand. Sex was selling; this was the era of the push-up bra. There would be multiple references to Dolce & Gabbana as *Sex and the City* dominated TV later in the decade, as Sarah Jessica Parker's Carrie Bradshaw ran off to Dolce & Gabbana parties around New York City and lusted after Dolce & Gabbana shoes in Manhattan windows.

RIGHT A very
Milanese Dolce &
Gabbana look for
A/W 1995/96.

OPPOSITE Linda
Evangelista walks
for S/S 1996 in all the
Dolce & Gabbana
hallmarks – animal
print, tailoring,
crucifix necklace.

The D&G line provided considerable financial stability. It was successful during its tenure, a mix of sportswear and vintage styles, youthful and contemporary, bright and fun. *Vogue on: Dolce & Gabbana* reports Kate Moss appeared on the front cover of *Vogue*'s October 1995 issue in a D&G microskirt. The line was a money winner, so the announcement that the label would close in 2011 baffled fashion and business commentators. The idea, apparently, was to merge it with the main line in a bid to strengthen the brand.

It was in 1994 that they debuted their first menswear fragrance, Dolce & Gabbana Pour Homme, as well as a new Home Collection shop featuring carpets, cushions, footstools and hand-painted ceramics. In 1995, the business signed a contract with Marcolin, the eyewear manufacturer, to launch a collection of men's and women's eyewear and in 1996, they would show their D&G collection in New York, their debut there. They also released a CD single, 'D&G Music'.

The empire was growing. Surprise trivia: it would further include the release of another CD, *D&G More More More*.

By now collections were expanding beyond the confines of Sicily and cinema, though these would always play a role. Just as the brand was going international, so too were its designs.

Spring/Summer 1997 was inspired by China and mixed prints and fabrics with all the Dolce & Gabbana signatures – leopard print and bustiers. Lines were long for dresses and overcoats that had something of a nightgown or nightdress appeal. It felt very vintage with faded florals and fuzzy trim on lapels and cuffs. The duo's ability to mix a host of references was developing, a collage of creativity, and the look was a memorable one of the late 1990s. Madonna wore this collection to the international premiere of *Evita* in 1996, while Nicole Kidman and Gwyneth Paltrow also wore pieces.

OPPOSITE *Vogue* editor Anna Wintour attends Dolce & Gabbana's 10th anniversary party in Milan, 1996.

OVERLEAF Lingerie looks for the S/S 1997 finale as the designers take their bow.

For Autumn/Winter 1997/98 and their collection Fellini/
Roma – The Vatican, the duo explored ideas around Italian
Catholic heritage. They referenced Fellini's film *Rome* as well
as Dino Risi's *The Priest's Wife*, all of which translated into
Edwardian silhouettes, dark and imposing. Accessories were
decorated and, according to the pair, a big hit; it was haunting
but sexy; surreal and ironically sombre.

For Spring/Summer 1998, a collection called Stromboli,
they switched things up, rejecting a big ready-to-wear show for
an intimate gathering akin to a couture. They had begun to
make pieces one by one on the mannequin and they wanted
their guests to be able to appreciate the details. The dresses
were complex and also beautiful – sheer and with butterflies
perched here and there, a little moody and sultry yet light.
It was a collection that, in retrospect, felt as though it was
heading to Y2K. Bright red, blue and yellow, the colour story
was striking. And there were little pedal pushers and scarves to
retain that Italian holiday feel.

As the millennium approached, the idea of the future and
hi-tech fabrications started to enter fashion's consciousness.
Dolce and Gabbana had always valued craftsmanship but they
were now keen to explore where they could take that with this
new age in mind. The collection for Autumn/Winter 1998/99
featured new fabrics, shiny and with liquid-like textures. Dolce
had always loved Balenciaga's proportions and here, they
were mixed with lots of florals – a tribute to Christian Dior, a
designer who had always loved flowers.

Prints were pretty, silhouettes lithe: Poiret-esque opera coats
brought back the past while shiny dresses, skirts and corsets
propelled them into the future. Looking back, it feels typically
1990s Dolce & Gabbana.

The same could not necessarily be said for the next

OPPOSITE D&G S/S
1997 was shown as
part of New York
Fashion Week.

OPPOSITE Kristen
McMenamy and
Domenico Dolce at
a Dolce & Gabbana
party, 1995.

BELOW Kyle
MacLachlan,
Domenico Dolce,
Linda Evangelista,
Stefano Gabbana,
Yasmin and Simon Le
Bon, 1995.

collection, Spring/Summer 1999 New Black – Hologram.
Apparently they fell out over this one, and Gabbana has said it's
here that you can see who is who when it comes to aesthetics.
Gabbana noted he was the cardigan, Dolce the jumpsuit.

The collection was full of new fabrics, techno-fabrics,
holographic fabrics. It was experimental, in line with what
many designers were doing as Y2K approached and the idea of
reinventing fashion – what it would be like in the future – took
them down some interesting pathways.

Reactions to this collection weren't so great, though.
Proportions felt off in a corset, jumpsuit and bolero
combination, which separately probably looked great. And there

was something disjointed to the collection, largely because of the fabrics, which lacked the heart and sentiment they were so good usually at portraying. However, as things turned out, everyone would be wearing those boleros: they became a huge Y2K trend.

Autumn/Winter 1999/2000 went kitsch. The collection was maximalist, full of print, colour, fur, fringe, everything together all at once. A backlash against the millennium minimalism that most designers had been predicting and/or courting.

Tops were tiny and beaded, belts were low-slung, thick and covered in sequins – again, these would be a huge trend and everywhere on the high street would also sell versions of them. This collection had a huge impact filtering down among the fashion food chain. Pink, orange, green, cerulean blue, everything said *touch me*, embellished and textured as it was — animal print, ruffles, more sequins, more beads. Jeans featured patchwork, skirts were lace and embroidered.

OPPOSITE The Dolce & Gabbana A/W 1999/2000 Ready-to-Wear collection.

It's around this time that they would also find one of their new muses: Gisele. They had met the Brazilian supermodel the year before. She was a new type of model. Glowing, athletic, sexy, strong in a way that hadn't been seen since the early 1990s and the supermodels. With grunge had come an extreme thinness, which lingered thereafter in fashion.

Gisele was hired for the campaign, photographed by Steven Meisel in Queens, New York. She would become part of the Dolce & Gabbana family (later becoming the face of a fragrance) and ushered in a new age of design as a new decade and the new century dawned. It felt younger, more modern, more fun — and of the time. The directly nostalgic element had been put away to let loose instead a host of mixing and matching, collaging together a new take on Southern Italy. A new Neorealism.

Their last collection of the 90s was shown in September 1999, Spring/Summer 2000 Mix and Match. It was exuberant, it was celebratory. They said they wanted women to feel like they could play with clothes. The idea was to be glamorous, creative and have fun.

And they did, with flowers, crystal mesh, diamonds, fringe, big buckles on tiny skirts — another lasting trend of the time — sheer shirts, Union Jacks in sequins, thick chokers, studding, hats and corsages — another hit trend; see *Sex and the City* — as well as platform wedge sandals and leopard print tights. Everything and more with a Swinging Sixties edge, the ultimate Dolce & Gabbana wardrobe.

OPPOSITE In
their Milan atelier,
complete with
animal print
background, in 1990.

RIGHT Amber
Valletta models
Dolce & Gabbana
S/S 1999.

THE DOLCE
& GABBANA
WARDROBE

A DISTINCTIVE STYLE REPERTOIRE

Liz Tilberis, the renowned former editor of British *Vogue*
and *Harper's Bazaar* US, once paid the brand a remarkable
tribute. In *10 Years of Dolce & Gabbana*, she explained
that she might see around 500 shows every season, and
among these Dolce & Gabbana's always stood out –
an impressive feat indeed.

And a very good indication that the brand had a real
and viable aesthetic as well as a product. Think of
Dolce & Gabbana, and a very specific and distinctive
series of garments comes to mind.

It includes corsets, bustiers and bras; little black dresses;
pinstripe and tailoring; flat caps; white vests; black lace; the
white shirt, unbuttoned just so and tied; exuberant prints
that might almost be souvenirs of Sicily; animal print; tiny
knickers; corsages; crochet, brocade and embroidery; shimmer
and shine; patchwork and collage. The list reads like the

OPPOSITE Prim with lace collars, a nod to Sicily here for A/W 2018/19.

contents of a wardrobe because it is – the Dolce & Gabbana wardrobe. More distinctive today than it ever has been.

Also a hallmark is the use of tradition to inspire the new, as well as the celebration of tailoring, craftsmanship and family – the culture of Italy. And while the duo has been creatively inspired by various eras, cultures and styles over the years (and indeed another of their trademarks is the ability to mix these together in a big, colourful patchwork), there are core pieces that have remained part of their style repertoire. And when you see them, you recognize them instantly.

Theirs is a DNA that has stayed constant. While the pair split personally in the early 2000s, they have continued to successfully work together, and so the brand has always been defined by the same two creative minds. They have grown together, come up with ideas together and had arguments together, but ultimately they have balanced one another and kept the brand in check – where other big Italian brands, even those with a longer heritage such as Salvatore Ferragamo, Pucci or Gianfranco Ferré, have gone through multiple creative heads and as such have disjointed periods of output.

The Dolce & Gabbana woman has always been glamorous, thanks to the muses who have inspired the designers. These include both of their mothers as well as the Italian actresses Anna Magnani, Sophia Loren and Monica Bellucci. This has filtered down into designs that have always been feminine, sensual, sexy and powerful. And while the duo have taken style notes from Neorealist cinema, they have never created costumes for it.

The late Franca Sozzani described the designers' style as largely omitting or obeying any rules, with each and every season being something of a surprise. Nor are they ever just retro when mining the past for inspiration. Such is their

own archive that they can now mine that for inspiration. As they recently did for the Spring/Summer 2024 womenswear collection. Titled Women, this was an ode to women of all ages and sizes and plundered their 1990s heyday.

As did the Re-Edition Spring/Summer 2023 show, a superb menswear collection that put the spotlight once more on the vest, a key component of the Dolce & Gabbana menswear wardrobe.

LEFT The pyjama collection for S/S 2009 – effortless but so chic.

OPPOSITE Jubilant jewellery and splaying skirts for S/S 2013.

OPPOSITE A white shirt, off the shoulder to reveal the bra, is among the ultimate of Dolce & Gabbana outfits. Here, A/W 2020/21.

BELOW Pinstripe, corset, cap, tie, tailoring – strong Dolce & Gabbana hallmarks for A/W 2020/21.

OVERLEAF The finale of S/S 2015 is among one of their many memorable – white shirts and red shorts. White shirts have played an important role in their depiction of sexiness.

It was a piece they had originally brought out with their debut menswear outing in the 1990s, having been inspired by Luchino Visconti's 1943 film *Obsession*, in which the protagonist wears a tank top, or vest (it would feature in many a costume of the genre). They pinpointed it as being the perfect combination of tradition and modernity – the garment itself is considered an undergarment and wasn't usually worn alone. Typically depicted on working-class men or peasants in neorealist films, it was particularly popular during the 1930s.

In their podcast, *Molto Italiano*, the duo suggest the tank top is for men what the bra is for women. The bras, bustiers and corsets are also a hallmark of their work. They featured early on, becoming more and more elaborate season after season.

Bras for Dolce & Gabbana have typically been styled peeking out from a little cardigan or underneath a white shirt, which is tied at the front and may be worn off the shoulder. Alongside

bejewelled bustiers and corsets, jackets and glittering dresses, they have also made for the impactful finale for which the brand has become well-known.

What Dolce & Gabbana has largely done is transformed undergarments into actual garments – even the Menswear Autumn/Winter 2023/24 collection featured corsets and girdles over slinky shirts on men. In womenswear, they have arguably become more va-va-voom than the early days. But there has been consistency.

LEFT A svelte and sinuous silhouette – Naomi Campbell walks for S/S 1997.

OPPOSITE Vintage, collage, patchwork, eclectic – Kate Moss models S/S 1997.

RIGHT For the hair?
Flowers, a tiara
or to emphasise a
neckline. Blooms for
A/W 2019/20.

OPPOSITE Gisele
does tailoring for
S/S 2000.

The brand's splaying petticoats – which took on epic and buoyant proportions for their Alta Moda show in 2023 – were originally inspired by a style that was popular in the late nineteenth century and which featured cords for lifting it to help the wearer to walk around.

A trimmed-down silhouette leans into their recognizable and somewhat dreamy summer dresses: often smothered in beautiful souvenir prints of fruit and florals inspired by traditional Sicilian carts.

Corsages have been used to emphasize a neckline or placed in the hair, a few at a time, to add further exuberance. There are signature trimmings in lace and crochet on necklines in a

throwback to a demure way of dressing. Crochet is an artisan technique that recalls the shawls of women in Southern Italy.

Accessories, over time, have become as starry as the clothes – and were Instagram fashion fodder before that even became a thing. There have been espadrilles and sexy stilettos, some boasting a D or DG as the heel, as well as spectacular pompom-festooned pumps and Sicilian print/sculpted sandals.

There is also the appropriately titled Sicily bag, the shape of a "proper" handbag, like something from the 1950s perhaps. It is smart and put together. The Dolce Box bag celebrates craftsmanship – some are embroidered, some bejewelled and others come in the shape of roses. These are bags able to play with novelty. The DG Logo bag makes for the ideal going-out bag, iterations ranging from fringe beading to statement embossed.

OPPOSITE
Accessories always stand out for the best reasons at Dolce & Gabbana – they are eye-catching and fun. Here, S/S 2018.

BELOW Sign of the times: the designers have never been afraid to embrace technology, and here, make a little fun of it with this bag for A/W 2017/18.

Crosses, which have sometimes been embellished with diamonds, speak of the pair's interest in religious iconography; and cameos were a feature of their early work.

Black is a Dolce & Gabbana shade, first featuring in their debut Geometrissimo collection and again in Trasformismo, before becoming a recurring and dominant tone into the 1990s. The Spring/Summer 1999 collection was New Black.

At other times, those catchy Sicilian Cart prints have dominated and you wouldn't know that black was such a favourite colour of the house. Likewise leopard print. But such is their affinity to the latter that at some point along the way, a compilation book was published celebrating their love of wild animal prints, as modelled by supermodels and superstars alike. Ask anyone what the words "Dolce & Gabbana" bring to mind and leopard print is likely to be among the top five.

It is this mix of conflicting elements that is also typically Dolce & Gabbana. Theirs is the ultimate patchwork.

OPPOSITE Kate Moss in leopard print, S/S 1997.

BELOW Lingerie looks have always been a part of the Dolce & Gabbana wardrobe. Here, making an impact for 2009.

LEFT Natasha Poly
walks for S/S 2012
in the kind of swishy
colourful, silhouette-
enhancing dress for
which the brand is
well known.

OPPOSITE Feminine
in florals for A/W
2015/16.

THE 2000s
AND
BEYOND

USHERING IN
A NEW ERA

Nostalgia for the early 2000s, or Y2K, has been palpable
among fashion trends for the early part of the 2020s.
Distressed denim, tiny tops, the resurgence of the corset,
slogans and logos, low-slung trousers, pop-style fashion.
A good many of these – corsages, bra tops, white vest tops –
Dolce & Gabbana were doing the first time around.

W hile the 1990s are considered the brand's heyday,
its success continued in the 2000s. Indeed, by
the turn of the millennium the brand reportedly
had annual sales above $300 million, and the duo owned an
estimated three residences in glamorous locations across the
globe. This was a world away from the little apartment and
the handful of lire with which they had begun.

The designers would explore the Italian side of the brand
less obviously and consistently through this new era. It was an
exciting time in fashion as creative minds considered what a

OPPOSITE Gisele looking powerful in a corset and lace for A/W 2007.

new century meant in clothes and when, following what is now largely considered a peaceful and prosperous decade, anything felt possible. Celebrity status had reached new peaks, reality TV was an emerging genre and somewhere in the background the internet was dialling up.

Dolce & Gabbana would find a new family member in Gisele Bündchen. At the time, the Brazilian beauty was the highest-paid model and epitomized the glamour and strength of Dolce & Gabbana for a new generation. Fashion was becoming more pop, more modern, more boho, and she wore it all well.

There would also be a new face, and a new look, in menswear. In the mid-to-late 2000s, Essex boy David Gandy would change the face of men's modelling after an affection for skinny and androgynous types thanks to Hedi Slimane at Dior Homme in the early 2000s.

Throughout this first decade of the new millennium, Dolce & Gabbana would experiment with a variety of styles and collections that notably had an impact on the high street; the idea of shopping online wasn't a thing yet (though shopping catalogues still were). Ribbon belts, thick embellished belts slung around the hips, billowing off-the-shoulder tops and corsages were all hits inspired by the brand.

The Autumn/Winter 2000/01 collection, Tamara de Lempicka, drew from the 1930s and the 1970s and featured Gisele in its campaign. With berets and long scarves, high necks and colourful tights and sparkle, it felt quite different to previous collections. The film star glamour was still there but in a more vintage and reserved fashion. Pleats and corsages, striped and spangly knits worn under entrance-making coats – the sweet spot of those two decades put together.

The duo would next turn their attention to the 1980s, which was starting to have a resurgence. They looked to the icons of

OPPOSITE Gisele models A/W 2001/02, when prairie tops and low-cut trousers were the order of the day.

the era for Spring/Summer 2001 and just as they did, rather fortuitously, the pop princess herself, Madonna, got in touch. She was working on her new album, *Music*, and wanted something Western to wear in a video for the song 'Don't Tell Me'. It just so happened they had pieces that matched her request.

They had been playing with body-conscious dresses with cutaways, tailored jackets and big shoulders. Eventually the show would dedicate a section to her. She would call again ahead of her press tour, this time wanting T-shirts with the names of her children in rhinestones. Also one that said "Kylie", in honour of the Australian pop icon, and one honouring "Britney", who had sung the US and UK into the millennium with her catchy tunes. Rhinestone T-shirts, it should be noted, caught on – big time.

Their next collection would become more boho. It was romantic and outdoorsy, with shearling gilets and corduroy fabric, items that again filtered into high street offerings. Jeans were bootleg, everything was quite furry and distressed and frayed. It ventured more into American West territory with Victoriana blouses and lace dresses – an aesthetic that was all the rage at the time. Domenico Dolce has even described it as being a little biblical. Possibly, but it was certainly popular: Jennifer Lopez, Kylie, Britney and Mary J. Blige all wore pieces.

Spring/Summer 2002's Latina collection brought stripes and ribbons and lots of colour. It is from this collection that little ribbon belts and billowing tops of paradise shades came to be first on everyone's shopping list. Trousers, too, featured stripes and kaleidoscopic patterns. It was an optimistic collection.

Autumn/Winter 2002/03 was more rustic – ponchos and fringing, tassels, studs, rope, leather, embellishment. Cargo pants with strappy sandals, blanket skirts, waistcoats. There were many accessories, too, because these had generally exploded onto the

OPPOSITE The D&G diffusion line, here for A/W 2000/01, was a huge success until it closed in 2011.

OVERLEAF Gisele, who became an ambassador for the brand in the 2000s, with the designers at the S/S 2002 show, in a very noughties look – an off-shoulder dress and ribbon-plaited belt.

fashion landscape and magazines would publish supplements dedicated to them, identifying the must-haves of the season.

For Spring/Summer 2003, in something of a crystal ball moment, the designers decided to look back at themselves and remake certain pieces (something which everyone is doing now in the 2020s). This vintage take on their own brand made up for the first half of the collection while the rest was a mix: a lot of white and silver, chainmail, chokers, striped shirts and embellishment.

Next season would go more romantic with florals and dresses designed with the Met Gala in mind but with an injection of techno, by which they meant ski jackets. There were flapper dresses and bejwelled columns and lots of colourful opaque tights, also a trend of the time.

But Spring/Summer 2004's Flower Power collection is one that particularly stands out. Everything was print. From every era and every pattern, it was mesmerizing. And the campaign, featuring models dressed in their florals and fauna among the autumn leaves, was a psychedelic treat for the senses. Daria Werbowy was photographed curled up at the bottom of a tree trunk in a layered dress with perfectly clashing tights. This was the point when printed tights really became a thing.

The designers would be inspired by Helmut Newton for the following collection, Autumn/Winter 2004/05. They had long admired the famed photographer, who died shortly after they began work on the collection. It was also, in some ways, an homage to Yves Saint Laurent. There were splashy fur coats over lace-edged lingerie, which all felt very 1940s and 1970s.

Next, they went to South Africa for Christmas, which got them looking at Richard Avedon and Irving Penn, both of whom had explored Africa. They looked at safari clothes, which in turn led them once again to Yves Saint Laurent.

OPPOSITE The designers at the beginning of a new century, dressing the part in distressed denim and Madonna *Music* T-shirts.

The overall impression for Spring/Summer 2005, they have said, was about a rawness and wildness. Animal prints featured heavily. As did sophisticated eveningwear.

Autumn/Winter 2005/06 marked 20 years since their very first catwalk show. And to celebrate they researched London, the Swinging London of the 1960s. David Bailey's images of Jean Shrimpton served as inspiration – it was all big coats, short skirts, straight shift shapes, stripes and belted macs. And the actress Chloë Sevigny made a surprise walk in the show.

Meanwhile it would become public knowledge in 2005 that the designers were no longer in a romantic relationship. They had apparently been separated for a couple of years prior with only close family and friends knowing.

People wondered how this would impact the business – but now, some 20 years or so on, it is clear that their split has not prevented them from having a successful and creative partnership. Indeed, the 2010s would see them enter one of their biggest and most expansive periods of creativity.

By the end of their 20th year in business, it was reported that they were now a billion-dollar brand and they celebrated the anniversary with a presentation for Spring/Summer 2006 that featured 98 looks and included spectacular gowns. Clearly for Dolce & Gabbana there lay an optimistic road ahead.

Spring/Summer 2007 saw Jessica Stam take to the catwalk in a corseted and armour-like mini ballgown – it would catch the attention of Lady Gaga, who wore it in the video and cover artwork for her song 'Paparazzi'. And Naomi Campbell memorably stepped out in a "chastity belt" look from their Autumn/Winter 2007 collection on the last day of her community service in New York. The collection itself had featured crystal embellished gowns, all cinched at the waist with chastity belts.

OPPOSITE Juliette Binoche was among those who turned out for the 20th anniversary celebrations of Dolce & Gabbana menswear in 2010.

And then along came David Gandy. In 2006, Gandy, who won a contract with a modelling agency through a nationwide competition, was picked by the designers and became the face of its Light Blue fragrance commercial in a pair of white Speedos alongside model Marija Vujović, photographed by Mario Testino.

It took the model stratospheric – and to a 15-metre (50-foot) billboard displayed in Times Square in New York (which, rumour has it, he never actually went to see). He would go on to make numerous appearances on the catwalk, often in similar Speedo styles, and be regarded as the first male supermodel.

Collections would next take a wander into the British countryside via Hitchcock for Autumn/Winter 2008 before a standout pyjama set collection in Spring/Summer 2009 – a little dog perched under the arm of one model, while Lily Donaldson wore a stunning princess dress for the finale.

The pair's greatest hits came next and therefore a look back to their forever inspiration. Titled Sicilian-ity Sartorial-ity Sensuality, Autumn/Winter 2010, it featured a giant parade of models at the beginning and end who took to the catwalk in black jackets and satin knickers. Dedicated to the brand's team of tailors, it was considered one of their most emotional shows – and this time there was very little in the way of set.

That would, of course, change for Autumn/Winter 2011. Then the audience was given the ability to send in texts and leave comments which were live-streamed onto screens above the catwalk. Dolce and Gabbana have never been shy of embracing technology, despite always keeping an eye on tradition. And indeed, Gabbana was well-known for being a fan of Twitter (now known as X). The trade title *Women's Wear Daily*, in its review of this show, noted there was no one more embracing of social media than them – at the time many designers were still on the fence (and a decade later, some still are).

OPPOSITE Showing off some muscle, David Gandy on the Dolce & Gabbana menswear S/S 2010 catwalk.

OVERLEAF Katy Perry performs at the D&G showroom in 2008.

RIGHT A/W 2008/9, a slightly 70s feel for D&G.

OPPOSITE Dolce & Gabbana S/S 2009.

The designers had already filled their Spring/Summer 2010 front row with bloggers (which had ruffled the feathers of the old guard) and in Spring/Summer 2016, models took selfies at the end of the catwalk. In Autumn/Winter 2017, the celebrity millennials, as they had been dubbed, had moved from the front row onto the catwalk as #DGMillennials.

Social media continues to play a key role in the brand today. Street style photographers swamp the outside of the Metropol show location in Milan, the tram lines adding that very Italian, very Dolce & Gabbana element to an otherwise standard stylish shot. And influencers, as well as the public, line it too. The latter, to catch a glimpse of the latest new, social media star. The former, in the hope of being photographed.

Amid all of this, the duo found themselves in the spotlight for an altogether different and not so great reason. In 2009, they were charged with tax evasion, a charge the two men denied, but the case would haunt them for the next five years until 2014, when Italy's highest court dismissed the case.

A better reason to be in the spotlight was the debut of a fine jewellery collection. The duo had long featured costume jewellery and bold, exuberant accessories – pasta earrings stand out – but in 2011, they ventured into fine jewellery. (It was a move that may well have served as a clue about what was coming next – couture.) The 80 pieces in the range were inspired by Sicily, naturally, and featured religious iconography.

Tradition and history would also come calling for the Autumn/Winter 2014 collection, which took a look at Sicily's Norman invasion, while Spring/Summer 2015 looked at when the Spanish ruled the island, the show ending with a catwalk finale of models in white shirts and little red shorts, led by Kendall Jenner.

OPPOSITE Natasha Poly in a signature hairband tiara for A/W 2012/13.

OVERLEAF Bianca Balti, right, and Natasha Poly, centre, in black and gold for A/W 2012/13.

Autumn/Winter 2015 was an Instagram moment and lent into the core family element of the brand's DNA. Mother's Day had seemingly come early in this collection which celebrated motherhood: babies, children and pregnant models took to the catwalk in pretty pieces featuring prints of what looked like children's sketches. And there were mini-me versions on offer, too.

Domenico Dolce's comments regarding family, though, got them into trouble the following year. Elton John called for a boycott of the brand following remarks surrounding IVF and gay families and protests took place outside Dolce & Gabbana stores. The designers apologized over what they later admitted were inappropriate comments.

A further controversy would hit in 2018 when the brand put out an advert featuring Chinese model Zuo Ye eating Italian food with chopsticks, which caused great offence and led to a severe backlash in China, where several retailers pulled the brand's products. The campaign came ahead of a show scheduled in Shanghai, which was subsequently cancelled. And comments alleged to have been made by Gabbana about China during an Instagram chat – which the brand said had been written by a hacker – didn't help matters.

But, the duo have also hit the headlines for their ability to embrace novelty. In 2018, one of their shows started particularly late as the audience was asked to turn the Wi-Fi on their phones off. This was peak social media time, so why exactly? The show began with eight drones carrying handbags down the catwalk before models made an appearance – digital audience participation in this instance, it was thought, would have disrupted the proceedings.

And in 2021, they released NFTs (non-fungible tokens), which had boomed amid the pandemic. On September 30,

Dolce & Gabbana sold a nine-piece collection of digital NFTs, as well as some actual couture for a staggering sum of 1,885.719 ether – a form of cryptocurrency, and the equivalent of nearly $5.7 million.

Buyers of these digital assets were reported as being leading NFT collectors. The brand had been approached earlier that year, it is reported, by the publisher of *Vogue Arabia*, who is also the founder of a company called UNXD. Dolce & Gabbana, ever the ones to try out new technology, had been taken by the idea. Five physical designs were produced with digital versions for the metaverse to accompany them.

Where would the brand go after this? A capsule collection, or rather a curation as it was dubbed, with Kim Kardashian came in 2022. The collection once again showing their ease at embracing an evolving world where social media and reality stars matter.

Bodycon, glitz, leopard print, crystal – this was about enhancing the power of women and drew on the brand's archive. Kim Kardashian, of course, is also known for her penchant for corsets. But for anyone who thought this might have been a quick trick, there is also the very serious and artisanal matter of Dolce & Gabbana's other business to take into account: Couture.

In 2011, the brand had closed the D&G line, which had been carried in 68 standalone stores and reportedly made up 40 per cent of the company's wholesale revenue. The decision was unexpected, but what the designers had up their sleeves was a much better surprise. And, in the long term, likely to make them far more money. By 2012, it became apparent that they were working on a new line: Alta Moda.

Building on the craftsmanship core of the brand, Alta Moda competed with the best of Paris. It was – and still is – Italian couture, pushing craft, technique and fashion dreams to the max. The Paris haute couture collections take place twice-yearly and are steeped in heritage and pride, available to only selected clients, and a handful of press – and now, influencers.

Dolce and Gabbana, however, decided they wanted to present their Alta Moda exclusively in Italy to spotlight their own country's artisans. The line debuted following a huge amount of secrecy, with only a handful of images given to the press. It would flourish and by the Autumn/Winter 2015 season, it was joined by a menswear counterpart, Alta Sartoria.

The designs have been inspired by masquerade balls, nature, flowers, dance, legends and more for collections that have taken clients to Milan, Capri, Portofino, Naples, Palermo and Venice on a tour of Italy and the Dolce & Gabbana world. The clothes are made to measure for clients and on each occasion have been spectacular: 4-metre (12-foot) trains, crystals, embroideries, pearls, pleats, splaying princess skirts –

BELOW The designers embarked upon a collaboration with Kim Kardashian for S/S 2023.

RIGHT Jennifer Lopez
at the brand's Alta
Moda show in Venice
2021, dressed in
Dolce & Gabbana.

everything they had ever done essentially on a far grander and more magical scale.

There is also a book dedicated to Alta Moda, conceived by the designers, titled *Queens*, which debuted in 2019 and features photographs of their friends and clients in their colourful couture.

In July 2023, a five-day Alta Moda event unfolded in Puglia. Some 500 guests attended the event which saw its narrow streets become part of the catwalk that led to an auditorium as locals stopped to watch – and in turn became a little like extras.

At a press conference before the show, Dolce claimed that these were clothes for cooking in. The huge, splaying skirts and

towering hats might have said otherwise. Regardless, it was a
production and collection that had been designed for the senses.

Italian artisans are not the only creatives Dolce and Gabbana
have supported. And while they themselves may now be part
of the established guard and globally known, they are also
supporting the new designers coming up. Just as they themselves
were given an opportunity way back when.

Recently, each season at the women's shows in Milan, they
have provided a platform for a young designer, with financial
and publicity support. They have supported Matty Bovan, a
Brit well-known for his colourful and wild creations, and Tomo
Koizumi, a Japanese designer known for his voluminous dresses
made from polyester organza. The latter drew inspiration from
the Dolce & Gabbana archive for his collection, resulting in
handmade flowers, iconic prints, ruffles, frills and colour. They
have also supported Miss Sohee, a South Korean designer who
takes a sustainable approach to looks using upcycled fabrics,
which came at a time when the company was actively declaring a
commitment to sustainability and promoting "Made in Italy".

Karoline Vitto, a Brazilian designer based in London, is a body
positive designer celebrating the female body, and showed during
the collections for Spring/Summer 2024. Walking the catwalk in
black, figure-hugging knitwear was Ashley Graham, who often
walks for Dolce & Gabbana. Other brand overlaps included the use
of bras and leopard print, and afterwards Gabbana was reported as
having been incredibly encouraging about Vitto's powerful designs.

But what of their own? The most recent Dolce & Gabbana
shows have themselves been noted by both the designers and the
press as a return to their roots. Sharp tailoring, black and white,
classic – all the ingredients are still there. Some 40 years after
their debut, they continue to be a fashion powerhouse.

The question is: where will they go next?

INDEX

CREDITS

The publishers would like to thank the following sources for their kind permission to reproduce the pictures in this book.